司马光

Heroes and Role Models | Non-Fiction Series

Copyright © 2022 by Level Learning, INC. and Washington Yu Ying PCS™
Original and Edited Text Copyright © 2022 by Washington Yu Ying PCS™

All rights reserved. No part of this book in whole or part may be reproduced without written permission from the publisher.

Published by Level Learning, INC.

Content Contributors:
Washington Yu Ying PCS™
Level Learning - Ya-Ching Chang

Illustrations by: Josh Taira

Leveling classification based on Level Learning standard. For full description, visit www.levellearning.com

ISBN 978-1-64040-004-7
Simplified Chinese Edition

About Level Learning:
Level Learning provides a literacy focused curriculum specifically designed for K-12 Chinese as a Second Language classrooms. Our program offers 20 levels of specific and detailed objectives, leveled texts and passages, mastery-based online assessment, and analytics to enable data-driven instruction. Level Learning reading curriculum for both literature and informational text emphasize grammar and comprehension skills to help teachers develop confident and independent Chinese language readers. The non-fiction series of books are specifically designed to support our informational text course based on multiple national standards. To learn more about our entire offering, visit www.levellearning.com.

About Washington Yu Ying PCS™:
Washington Yu Ying PCS is a Mandarin English dual language immersion International Baccalaureate (IB) World school. Yu Ying's mission is to inspire and prepare young people to create a better world by challenging them to reach their full potential in a nurturing Chinese/English educational environment. Yu Ying's comprehensive IB, dual immersion curriculum equips students with global competencies for success in the real world. As a leader in immersion education, Yu Ying is determined to advance Chinese language programs and global citizenry education by helping other schools create and strengthen their Chinese programs. For more information, email: products@washingtonyuying.org

司马光，宋朝人，出生于1019年。他是中国古代著名的历史学家。

司马光从小就对历史非常感兴趣，在他的书架上经常放满了许多跟历史有关的图书。他每天都会花很长时间阅读这些书。

司马光非常聪明，遇到难题时喜欢思考，找到解决问题的办法。在他小时候，有一次他和朋友们一起在院子里玩，突然一个朋友不小心掉进了水缸里。其他的孩子都吓得大哭，不知道该怎么办。

只有司马光没有哭,他冷静地用石头砸破水缸。就这样,掉进去的孩子被救了出来。

长大以后,司马光还是认真努力地学习历史,把自己的才能用到和历史有关的事情上。

《资治通鉴》是司马光写的一套非常有名的历史书。这套书里讲了16个朝代，一共1362年的历史。

在编这套书的时候,司马光经常忙得忘记吃饭,很晚才睡觉。每次遇到难题,他都会努力地找出答案。

因为司马光做事认真,他花了十九年的时间,才终于完成了这套书。直到现在,《资治通鉴》在中国的历史书中都有着非常重要的地位。

Glossary

	Pinyin	English Definition
宋朝	sòng cháo	Song dynasty
著名	zhù míng	famous
历史学家	lì shǐ xué jiā	historian
历史	lì shǐ	history
兴趣	xìng qù	interest
书架	shū jià	bookshelf
有关	yǒu guān	related
书	shū	books
阅读	yuè dú	to read
聪明	cōng míng	smart, intelligent
难题	nán tí	problem
思考	sī kǎo	to think, to reflect
解决	jiě jué	to solve
突然	tū rán	suddenly
水缸	shuǐ gāng	water tank

	Pinyin	English Definition
吓	xià	scared
冷静	lěng jìng	calm, cool
砸破	zá pò	smash
救	jiù	to save
认真	rèn zhēn	serious
努力	nǔ lì	hardworking
才能	cái néng	talent
一套	yí tào	a set, a series
朝代	cháo dài	dynasty
忘记	wàng jì	to forget
答案	dá àn	answer
终于	zhōng yú	finally
完成	wán chéng	to complete
地位	dì wèi	rank, place

www.ingramcontent.com/pod-product-compliance
Lightning Source LLC
Chambersburg PA
CBHW041224070526

44584CB00001B/85